UNSTUCK

Also by the same author:

Alphabet Soup for Grown-Ups

At Left Brain Turn Right

Book the F*cking Job

Book the Job (For Teens)

You Knew When You Were Two

UNSTUCK

A Life Manual On How To Be More Creative, Overcome Your Obstacles, and Get Shit Done

by Anthony Meindl

edited by Barbara DeSantis

Edited by Barbara DeSantis

Cover and book design by Kathryn Lejeune

ISBN 978-0-578-37294-5

This book is dedicated to all the Artists. May you continue to pursue your creative dreams and not give up. The world, I think, keeps rotating on its axis because of your passion and work.

ACKNOWLEDGEMENTS

This book is only possible because of the support and hard work of so many people behind-the-scenes. Thanks to my editor, Barbara, for her encouragement and dedication. Sharon, for her early enthusiasm for this work and everything I am writing. Katie, for believing I had another book to write. Kathryn, for her incredible design skills and book knowledge. Jenn, for her ongoing work to share this book to all those who might be interested, and Lauren for her incredible proofreading eye.

Robin, for being the Officer of All Things, which has helped create our own little Hogwarts and all the faculty and staff and students of AMAW Studios worldwide. The work we are all doing, collectively, helps further this work and these ideas; inspires and uplifts and continues to take creating into a New Age.

And for Howin, my heart, thank you.

INTRODUCTION
The Problem Is In The Premise.

There are so many problems in life right now it's a wonder any of us get out of bed in the morning.

There's climate change. And conspiracy theories. And of course, conspiracy theories *about* climate change.

There's systemic racism and the social justice movement's revealing how people of color have been marginalized and prejudicially treated for decades. From redlining to school districting; from job inequality to police brutality.

There's immigration policy and the national debt.

There's Covid and the millions of people who have died from it. And there are Covid-deniers, and the denial that millions of people have died from it.

There's zoonosis and pandemics and bacterial pathogens becoming increasingly resistant to antibiotics. There are vaccines, and mind-boggling theories claiming that getting one comes with a microchip being covertly implanted in your arm.

There is Facebook misinformation and the growing number of people who get their news *only* from Facebook misinformation. There are online trolls and cyberbullies.

There is Russian meddling in our elections and the threats of voting fraud *before* voting has taken place.

There are voting rights at risk as well as women's rights being violated. There are transphobic acts of violence, homophobia, and anti-Asian and anti-Muslim hate groups. There are civil wars, and domestic abuse, and homelessness, and an opioid epidemic, and gun violence.

And the list goes on. And each of us contends with these outer conflicts—how they disrupt our lives and create division, conflict, pain and chaos—in our own way. And they bleed into (and often affect) our own interpersonal conflicts. They may ignite long-simmering resentments or outright rage. They may break apart an old wound barely being held together or dredge up previous trauma.

Unresolved skirmishes, in our minds and on the battlefields of life, may resurface against our siblings, parents, ex-lovers, teachers and friends. And against ourselves.

Conflict, in short, is everywhere.

We are conflicted about our art and performance, about our careers and relevancy, about doing things that are worthwhile, and making money. We are conflicted about our life's dreams and what matters, about the meaning of it all and our innate purpose. We are conflicted about dating and love and fame and America and aging and marriage and death.

With so much conflict—both internally (psychologically, emotionally, spiritually) and everywhere else in the world—is it no wonder we want to disconnect, disengage, turn off and shut down?

As if that's not bad enough, we constantly are bombarded with erroneous messaging that a "problem-free" life is that which we should aspire to have. That all the "greats"—rich and famous people and those living the glamorous lives—are free of petty conflicts, and that money, fast cars, beautiful friends, vacations in Mykonos, and being popular is the panacea that eradicates our pain.

By comparison, our lives look like an episode of a bad soap opera. Messy, dramatic, riddled with failures and beset by daily challenges that don't seem to go away. Obviously—our thinking goes—all our problems must mean we're doing something wrong and aren't cut out to be doing whatever it is that we want to do.

But the problem is in the premise.

Most of us are taught that the goal in life is to achieve some sort of nirvana. Amassing 1 million (or is it 2 million?) followers, have perfect abs, take dream vacations where we step from our private bungalows into pristine blue ocean waters, create a whole line of beauty products and best-selling books, own a vacation rental, have a perfect spouse and instagram-worthy children who have their own accounts of millions of fans.

And, oh, it's also supposed to be devoid of missteps, mistakes, failures, challenges, and obstacles, and we're supposed to look young and fabulous and hot and *happy* while arriving at some Holy Grail of spiritual enlightenment, a career pinnacle success and outward achievement that proclaims we're "the best".

We have finally made it! *Yeehaw*. Instagram says it's so. Now comes the good stuff. Now is the time of parties on yachts, and day-tripping to Ibiza and having no cares and being free of the challenges that the *losers* have to deal with every day. Like cleaning a stinky cat litter box and looking at an expanding waistline in the mirror; waiting on hold for a customer service representative to tell us our credit card is maxed out while doing the dishes.

Now for sure, money can make *some* of these things go away by hiring other people to clean your stinky cat litter box—but it doesn't mean new, different, equally complicated problems won't arise in their place.

A rich/successful/famous/influencer/hot person's problems may seem to be those of the "champagne" variety... but they're still problems, nonetheless.

Conflict though, as tremendously painful and challenging as it is, is also a necessary source for our creative breakthroughs and life victories. From a cultural standpoint—the passing of Civil Rights legislation, to women's rights, to LGBTQIA2+ rights and the creation of labor unions—to the personal; a reconciliation with a long-lost family member, an engagement, a career achievement or an improvement in one's health—conflict *evolves* us.

Conflict gives birth to solutions and ideas, real creativity and oftentimes life-altering technology, scientific findings, health breakthroughs, and art that inspires and uplifts, as well as interpersonal healing, spiritual progress and greater intimacy.

In short, with everything that we collectively and personally face, there would be no expansion and awareness without conflict.

So, how do we learn to become less ensnared in any specific conflict per se, and instead use it to create, fight for things that matter, find a more authentic and passionate voice, and use it to support the causes that mean more wins for everyone and ultimately leave you (and culture) a better place because of your ability to not give up?

Let's examine some ideas, myths and beliefs around our fear of—and need for—conflict in life and realize there isn't something wrong with you because you seem to face it. *A lot.*

Like a shit-storm every week, it seems.

In fact, it means just the opposite.

There is no problem-free life except in death. (Or not trying.) And because death hasn't happened to us yet, let's get going with what life wants to show us—how to conquer our artistic goals through the wonderful, weird, perfectly orchestrated yet seemingly chaotic construct of conflict in your life.

Let the shit-storms begin!

The Beginning.

Life—whether you think in terms of the Cosmic Big Bang or God's Biblical version of the Big Bang—was not without problems. It was inherently full of chaos. Order took form out of this disorder over hundreds of millions of years (or metaphorically, the Biblical version was a speedy seven days!) but that occurred through the mighty, dramatic confrontations that occurred in the process.

Noxious, poisonous gases ruled the planet. No oxygen in sight. Volcanic gaseous and methane particles inhibited life forms (at first) from evolving. Eventually, over hundreds of millions of years, through photochemical production and photosynthesis, the first eukaryotic organisms were born.

Over time, more simple organisms and cellular microbes originated—who were, in turn, devoured by a predatory cousin here, and a rogue virus there. Yet, all of this wild unfolding occurred only in the seas, mind you. Nothing terrestrial had yet been born.

It wasn't until around 400 million years ago that the first tetrapod (think ancient salamander!) was brave enough to say, "Land, Ho!" and venture forth onto dry land risking really dry skin and other challenges—like not being able to walk well—only to be eaten millions of years later by other, bigger, more advanced terrestrial and avian creatures.

And for millions of years evolution went on like that.

Creation. Conflict. Obstacles. Problems. Challenges. Setbacks. Evolution.

And then we arrived.

Neil Armstrong said after his moon landing, "That's one small step for man, one giant leap for mankind."[1]

Sorry, Neil. The biggest step for mankind was the creative process that moved us from the sea to the beach!

Without that tetrapod going bravely where no tetrapod had ever gone before, you and I simply wouldn't exist. We owe everything to these heroic, early amphibious buggers.

Giant leaps, indeed.

Later on, Charles Darwin coined this struggle *Survival of the Fittest*.

But maybe, surviving through conflicts over resources for water, and food, and reproduction, and territory (as Darwin hypothesized) also suggested a sort of *agreement*: an unconscious *dance* that participants have signed up for in order to evolve and survive together.

A lion *seems* to be the winner because he eats the gazelle and is on top of the food chain. But the number of times the lion fails in even capturing a gazelle is more than 70-75%. (And that's with having an *entire* pride trying to ambush their prey.)

This means, over time, more and more gazelle outnumber the lions and therefore prosper and flourish. But too many gazelle mean too little grass for other herbivores, so the lion is also a part of the solution—not just the problem for the gazelle— but also part of the agreement that is made. A lion takes the weakest or oldest from the herd, thereby removing possible genetic deficiencies that could be passed from generation to generation and affect the herd's overall health.

We humans also engage in these unconscious agreements with others, and with our art, history, stories, culture, animals, nature, and what we almost often forget—agreements within ourselves during the creative process. This interplay between tension and problems—creating and finding solutions—is a push-pull born within ourselves. The *Big Bang* isn't just out there somewhere in the cosmos, the *Big Bang* chaos is going on inside us too.

It's necessary.

The solutions to our creative problems are inherently embedded within the obstacles. Without the problems there would be no creativity. Period.

Like life itself, our own evolution involves facing the problem right in front of us, and realizing it is also there for our benefit. So let's take a look at how to hack the problems that we face on our creative journeys and not, perhaps, think of them so much as problems but instead *as opportunities.*

Sort of how those fearless tetrapods saw leaving the oceans to venture forth to new lands and new adventures.

Conflict Conceives
Creativity.

Born out of the void, here for moments in time (and out of time) and then gone.

This can apply to ourselves, our loved ones, ideas, epiphanies, and the genesis of creativity itself.

Do some people have more creative talent than others? Can it be cultivated? Nurtured? How do we access more of it in our own life? And most importantly, how do we get out of its way? Are we even *in* the way? Or are our innumerable self-imposed roadblocks to it, also, simultaneously the path to more of it?

Can *what's in the way* actually be *the way?*

And what are the steps needed to find our way?

Are children naturally plugged into something—a creative force—that disappears as we get older and "smarter" (i.e., jaded, sarcastic know-it-alls)?

How do we recapture the childlike *essence* that abides within us but also seems to come from someplace *else*? It's *here* and yet not here. Or rather, the location is hard to find.

The great Theatre director Jerzy Grotowski called his process of creativity *Via Negativa*.

The negative path.

In short, it was a philosophy built on a belief that the art of acting wasn't about a "collection of skills but (instead) an eradication of blocks."[2] That is, by eliminating the obstacles that stifle or block a person's creative expression is what allows that artist to become free.

It was a way of describing something by saying what it is not.

Until we get the obstacles *out of the way*, the obstacles *are the way*.

But weirdly, the obstacles are part of the process *needed* to reveal the artistry.

So what stops you is also the momentum that is trying to force you to keep going.

We stop because we think there's something wrong with us when we start bumping up against challenges. We give up because we think the "greats" haven't faced the same hardships we have. We throw in the towel because we interpret setbacks as a sign from the universe that we aren't gifted, or deserving or meant to be doing this.

But what if those obstacles are the very things that create the idea, the inspiration, the "Ah-Ha", the *art* that finally answers

5

some of your life's questions? Finally gets you past the finish line? Finally shows you that without those tribulations, the triumph perhaps was impossible?

When something not so wonderful happens in your creative journey, it doesn't mean it's unwanted.

Well for sure no one wants it. (Unless you are a masochist who enjoys the pain of it all!) It'd be a hell of a lot easier if it just wasn't there, but if you sit down and examine this thing, hear what it has to say, invite it to lunch, let it reveal to you what you're scared of and what's *really* holding you back, you might be surprised with what you discover.

The tension, the friction, the *fight* is the actual stuff that unlocks your creative breakthroughs.

For many of us artist-soul-types, the negativity we often associate with the setbacks is what makes the journey such a slog. But if you start to understand how it works, stay in the game, keep participating enthusiastically, stop taking things so personally, do more of the things you wish to see and do… eventually you will get to the other side and will have something to show for it.

So, let's take a look at some core concepts and how we shift out of a negative headspace of what occurs when we feel defeated, and how to make that thing we struggle against the *very* thing that can help us. It truly is possible.

Conflict Is Not Resistance.

So, to recap: conflict is a *normal* aspect of life on a rogue planet in the middle of outer space.

Good to know.

To be in the natural flow of conflict is to arrive at *conflict resolution* because conflict will eventually resolve itself. It also requires a certain amount of emotional intelligence and awareness. Things arise because of the conflict—things are brought to light that had you not engaged in the discomfort of conflict, you probably wouldn't be conscious of.

For example, in relationships, what might be revealed is your tendency to shut down when intimacy occurs.

In creativity, it might be your habit of not finishing things as a way to keep yourself from rejection.

In family dynamics, it might be assuming a childhood role because that feels most comfortable and safe.

Whatever the example, our internal *and* external conflicts are trying to show us *patterns* and serve both a biological evolutionary function, as well as awaken our spiritual evolution and awareness.

So, to avoid conflict is to avoid our own growth.

But conflict is not resistance.

Resistance is a *negative response or reaction to* conflict.

Conflict is normal. Resistance is not.

If conflict is hard enough to face and navigate, why on earth would we want to add more resistance to it?

Well, because it's scary, and we naturally want to resist something that feels uncomfortable.

If, instead of resistance, however, we surrendered to—or accepted—and acknowledged our own resistance to conflict, we would naturally be led to catharsis, healing, and problem solving.

This is because solutions will be born *out of the problem* as long as we don't *fight* the problem.

Don't do extra work.

Accepting resistance doesn't mean ignoring or condoning bad behavior. It doesn't mean allowing bad things to happen when you have the power to change those things. It simply means understanding it at a level that allows you to take action to change it, resolve it, or heal through it.

It's an *art* of surrender. An *art* of acceptance. And there is a real art to working through something that many people would rather pretend isn't there.

So, the next time you feel the juggernaut of conflict heading your way, don't brace for impact. Get in there and work with it.

If you're not having any conflict in life, you're not really living your life. (Which at some level is statistically impossible, because, again, *conflict* is a natural part of life.) But the consistent avoidance of it reflects our not wanting to take risks, play, put ourselves out there, make mistakes and fail.

But ultimately succeed.

To conflict doesn't mean to err. It means you're in the creation game.

So bless that mess.

Stop Making Things Harder.

Getting *in the way* of flow is what makes accessing creativity hard.

Oh, and also because we're all a bunch of liars.

I lie to myself. My parents. I've lied to boyfriends, and cheated on geometry tests. (Which is a form of lying because everyone thinks I earned the "A" myself.) I've lied about my age more times than I care to remember. (Age is a number and mine is *unlisted!*) I've lied on resumes and job interviews. I've lied when I've had too much to drink or want to check out emotionally. I've lied about being in denial about lots of things I've lied about.

I've even lied to myself about how much I've lied.

What creating is asking us to do is be more honest with ourselves in our work than we often are normally in our daily lives, because we're so good at lying. And that requires a real, radical look at oneself.

And what we discover is that, if we meet ourselves at the center of our art, no matter what it is, right there in that place, there is no escaping the truth. And it might give us the permission to be even more honest in life, too. That's art's purpose.

Thank god for art then. It makes us more honest. To ourselves and to the world. We need more artists. They aren't necessarily better at telling the truth. They're just forced to do it if they want to create honest work.

Getting more honest with ourselves, then, will naturally make things less hard. We will stop giving energy to resisting parts of ourselves that we lie about and judge. (More on this later.)

Wouldn't it be more fun and easier to just come clean? Certainly something we can all try to do more of. Like the marionette Pinocchio, as we become more brave and truthful, we go through a metamorphosis that opens up our lives to becoming more fully human and alive.

Michelangelo + David.

There is the story about how Michelangelo sculpted his masterpiece *David* by chipping away what wasn't the man. He had a huge slab of marble brought in from Bologna (*Hold the Baloney!*) or somewhere, and staring at a huge block of stone, he chipped away pieces here and there, removing chunks above and below, until what remained was the Art.

The David.

You. Me. Creation.

What remains when we get rid of all the bullshit blocking our way—or rather what we put in our own way—is us.

The artist. The perfection as we are. The mirror.

We are both the Michelangelo and the David.

Inside the cold, hard marble block that encases you, hides you, and protects you is an even more perfect beautiful form called you.

Your job is to reveal *that* part of you. Uncover yourself. Disrobe. Get naked. Get real. Just like the David. And what the world will see is an incredible piece of art.

But remember, the removal of the unwanted marble is what reveals the David. Without this process of eliminating the excess, there is simply no art to admire.

Making Art Isn't Precious.
(So Get Over Yourself.)

Creating isn't devoid of missteps and blow-outs.

It's a process.

You have to blow things up. Wreck stuff. Kill your darlings.

When kids make a *Play-Doh* castle, they enjoy constructing an imaginary world.

Then they demolish it. Rip it apart. Combine all colors of clay into a mash-up that turns the *Play-Doh* grey.

It's creative. And fun.

It's also a messy process.

So much for preciousness.

Create. Destroy. Design. Demolish. Try. Attempt. Fail. Play. And try again. Step and repeat.

I'm Stuck.

No you're not. You're scared. Don't confuse the two.

There's a solution to every stuck. What you choose to do with that is what either *unsticks* you or not.

Let me repeat. For every problem that exists, there is also a solution.

If I'm stuck, and I move, I'm unstuck.

You could argue, "Well what if I can't move? What if I'm stuck and I literally can't move?"

Then *ask for help!*

There is always someone to help us. A teacher. Friend. Preacher. Lover. Brother. Sister. Parent. Paramedic. Telephone operator. Dog handler. Grocery clerk. Trainer. Truck driver. Cabbie. Waiter. Referee. Coach. Neighbor. Tour guide. Passerby. Flight Attendant. A stranger. God.

Siri.

So ask.

I'm Blocked.

Start small.

If you know you're blocked you're not blocked.

Awareness unblocks you.

So what do you *do* with that awareness? You *speak* about the block.

You tell your parents, "So here's where I have problems." Or you say to your lover, "Here's what's hard for me," and that immediately moves you toward unblocking the stuff.

You share yourself with someone you can trust. "I sometimes question my sanity."

You get honest and vulnerable with a friend. "I don't think I'm cut out for relationships."

You reveal your fears to a sibling. "I get scared a lot but don't want to admit it."

If you aren't even aware that you're scared, chances are you'll be back to being *stuck*.

Then all you have to do is follow the steps to get *unstuck* and on you go.

These are the steps to life. And everyone takes them. Up, up we are going. Just try to leave the kicking and screaming at the bottom, thank you.

Have you ever had a problem and discussed it with a good friend? Instead of focusing on your problem, they see your potential. They believe in your talent. They see a way out.

There are two keys to this example. First, you actually *told a friend*. That's important. As we discussed, what's scary needs to be shared. And second, your friend doesn't really spend a lot of time talking about the problem. They immediately hone in on solutions.

What would happen if you started seeing your problems the way your friends see them? Just a temporary challenge you are overcoming on the way to being unblocked.

I'm Lost.

It depends on where you *think* you're going, how you think you have to get there and what you think the destination is supposed to look like.

By those standards, we're all "lost".

No one, and I mean no one, is certain of anything since we're all visitors to this planet. Surviving a plague and living through a pandemic has made some of us wake up to the fact that we have no control, and at its core, *all* of life is uncertainty.

Home is not here on this planet.

If this is not our home, then to find permanent residence here seems ill conceived.

You find home by embarking on your hero's journey (as philosopher Joseph Campbell calls it), which is simply walking your path.

We often think, "If I had just done it like everyone else, I'd have been fine." Or, "I don't even trust myself." Or, "If I become an Influencer, my life will be perfect." Or, "Everyone else seems to have it figured out!"

No one knows! No one has figured it out!

Not the church or government. Not your boyfriend or teacher. No TikTok star or sports icon. No celebrity or podcaster. Not even your parents.

So really, being *lost* is also a by-product of *believing* that everyone else has the recipe for the secret sauce.

Which can eventually make you feel *stuck* (see previous chapter).

As our Neanderthal cousins (more on them later) understood life—*The journey was the destination.* Or perhaps they even understood it, being nomadic, at an even deeper level.

There is *only* the journey.

No destination.

Just journeys.

I Have No Credits.
I Have only 137 Followers.
I've Never Been Published.

Start where you are.

People who have no credits get credits by doing things.

People whose art hangs in galleries aren't more talented than you. It just means they've been busy making art.

Writers who get published, wrote the book.

Worry less about credits and just get working. When you start creating you won't care about credits because the actual art of making things is the credit itself.

Deciphering The Lie.

Once we've "made it," or have more money, or are famous, or have more security we'll be in a better position to create or do the things we really want to do. Our life will *finally* begin.

That's the lie.

Status, comfort, notoriety, money, more "fans" or followers have nothing to do with creativity.

You are inherently creative without those things.

Creativity comes first.

There is nothing inside you right now that you are missing that you think you *need* to be creative.

If You Don't Have A Philosophy... Make One Up Now.

It's good to have one. I would say you essentially *need* one to survive life.

It can be anything. That's where religion comes in handy, if it's not dogmatic, and shame-based, and judgy, and excludes everyone who doesn't believe in that same religion. (So, yikes, that criteria might eliminate a lot of religions.)

Maybe it's faith.

But desserts can be a good philosophy too.

Pie. Cherry, apple, or blueberry pie is a *great* philosophy to live by.

So is exercise or meditation, or loving film. Friendships.

Spending time in nature. Coffee. Writing poetry. I went through a period where *cereal* was my religion! It got me through a lot of challenges.

Filmmaker John Cassavetes said that a philosophy is that which is driven by love.[3]

Let something bigger than you move you through life.

Inspire you. Keep you tethered to what's real, and important, and true. Create a practice by which you live your life. A mantra may be born out of it.

One that I like to remember:

Is what I'm about to say going to uplift and inspire this person?

Is it true?

If not, keep your mouth shut.

We would all be so much quieter.

Just Because Our Minds Tell Us Something Is True, Doesn't Make It So.

Our minds.

It's so ironic we spend so much time there.

Yet that's exactly where most of our pain originates.

Faith.

Faith is the substance of a thing hoped for; evidence of a thing yet unseen.[4]

That's what the Bible says. I'm not a theologian, but I always loved that phrase because to me, it's also a bit scientific.

Here's why.

To have faith gives us the raw material to visualize our dreams and give birth to them. In other words, you can see yourself winning an award, or writing that novel, or sculpting your own *David*.

It's not mind over matter, it's mind *into* matter.

Faith is the substance. It's the substrate. The soil. The fertilizer *and* the nutrients.

Faith broken down into a smaller incremental element can be considered as *thinking*. Thoughts are things—*As a man thinketh.* When I *think* about things, I create more energy around the things I'm thinking about.

At a collective level this happens all the time. The more energy (in terms of conversations or retweets or reposts) we give to something, the more people are attracted to it, taking it to a more visible level. It becomes a phenomenon. It goes "viral". (Which we will explore later isn't always a good thing in terms of social media.)

Evidence?

This is where it gets tricky. To have evidence in faith is impossible, because it's unseen and unknowable. But still, there it is. By my having faith that the things I can imagine *can* come true, that is the evidence I need for those things to come true.

To have faith is simply to have a belief in *something*. It's not unlike having a philosophy, which in many ways it is.

The word faith is derived from the Latin *fides*, from the root of *fidere* "to trust."[5] So, isn't it also trusting in what you're setting out to do?

But you don't have to have faith in the Divine or God or a Creator to experience dreams coming true. Your faith can come in doing good work. It can come in the work itself. It can come in terms of service or giving back.

A belief in the power of making art as a practice, builds faith. And it builds faith in oneself.

That belief forges your work. That belief in the *power* of what you are doing is what creates faith. And there's faith in the ancillary things that come from the things we do too.

Perhaps in the *big* scheme of our *short* lives, the things we do ultimately have little significance. But the community they establish, the relationships they afford, the inspirations and assistance they bring, the joy and connection they evoke, *these* are the things to have faith in.

Fellowship.

Friendship. Love. People. Collective. Community.

These things build our faith, and help us to endure and create more committed, deeper things to believe in.

Don't believe it because the Bible says it. Believe it because the belief will make it so.

All it takes is a little faith.

The Imposter Syndrome.

This word is very popular nowadays. I never heard of it when I was in my twenties. But like all these buzzy phrases that social media has made popular, it's taken hold. Sort of like those annoying tech words like "pivot" or "synch up" or "leverage" or "visibility".

Very catchy, trendy words that are more cool than they are substantive.

This idea that you're undeserving, a fraud—that you're not as smart or talented or "together" as people might think makes you an "imposter" and therefore unqualified in whatever it is you want to do and someday you're going to be found out.

By whom? The imposter police?

You're not an imposter, you're a human being.

Or maybe a better way of thinking about it is that if you are one, then you are as much of one as everyone else.

We're *all* imposters.

We're all making things up. We all start out from scratch. From nothingness. Literally. We all gain skills and understanding as we go along. We're all riding the wave of life without a map and a compass. Or maybe we have maps and compasses but we still get lost.

Perhaps, as we forge forward in our lives, we acquire more information and knowledge. We hopefully make better choices and become more compassionate. And yet still we wing it half the time.

In the end, life is truly about living on a *wing and a prayer*.

Because you're new to something, or just starting out, or the world hasn't celebrated you yet, doesn't mean you're a fake.

Imposter syndrome is created by a scared mind that is convinced everyone else knows something that you don't. And that the only way you are ever going to "make it" is by knowing as much as those people you attribute as knowing. And that the "knowing" comes from other people anointing you, or liking you, or "following" you, or crowning you successful or popular or talented. Or by doing it *their* way.

Money can really alter people's perception, too. Oftentimes, the people we think "know", got there because of money. Someone who makes a lot of money must "know" something we don't. Money just seems to make it so. If you're rich, you *must* know, otherwise you wouldn't have a lot of it.

See how that works? But what you might have discovered is that the people you think know – (even with lots of money) – actually don't either.

I'll say it again. No. One. Knows.

Some people are *really* great at pretending they do.

But the honest ones—the ones who *have* been doing something for a very long time and are probably really good at what they do—will tell you that they still aren't quite sure what it is that they're doing. Yes, you gain more experience as you traverse life, but no one ever has completely figured it out.

What also creates the imposter syndrome is when we compare ourselves to others. We look at what other people have accomplished and think we can't do it, or if we are doing it, it's not correct, *compared* to what they're creating. Therefore, there's something wrong with us. We believe that there's a problem that needs to be solved *before* we're deserving, or worse, even *before* we create. So half the time, we just don't create.

There is nothing wrong with you. Nothing needs to be solved. It's not a problem. Life isn't in error.

Life simply is.

All we can do is try to be more ourselves—and try less to be someone else—and discover that your imposter sits nicely in this world of fellow imposters and on we go from generation to generation and beyond. A world of make believers, pretending we all know some things, and in the end, we may discover we still know nothing.

I recently had a chat with my parents, who are both 86 (!), and asked them about what they had learned on their long, beautiful journey of life. Of course, they have had so many experiences and memories; challenges and defeats, and things they perhaps would have done differently. But the most surprising revelation was that in the end, really, what they learned is that they still know almost nothing at all.

And isn't that good to know? There's a freedom in that.

Something Is Wrong With Me...

Why?

Because someone hasn't hired you for a job? Because you haven't found your significant other? Because your agent dumped you and you can't get a new one? Because you got fired? Because you've been working hard for a long time with no tangible results to show for it? Because you can't get your book published, your painting sold, your song recorded?

Those experiences don't mean something is wrong with you. They're reminders that you are in the *conflict* of life and on your path.

None of the things we read, or watch, or listen to ultimately mean *anything* about us or where we are (or aren't) unless we give those things a negative association based on false assumptions accrued from misinformed childhood years. So, for example, a pop star's latest hit doesn't mean you won't have a hit too at some point. Her success doesn't mean you are destined for nothing.

When we compare ourselves, we buy into social media posts

proclaiming that the loudest, prettiest, most fantastic, successful lives look a certain way. Ours don't look like that, so we must be failing. Or because we haven't hit the expectations and definitions of what we have been told "success" looks like, we are losers.

There's not something wrong with us because we are (metaphorically) the last to get chosen for high school scrimmage games in gym class. (I hated that, by the way, and I often thought there was.) And when we make an incorrect assumption based on *why* we weren't chosen, our traumatized eight-year-old self is being triggered, making a false association between being "chosen" and our value.

There's nothing wrong with us when things aren't going our way. Or because we're the last to be chosen. Or we aren't chosen at all.

A prayer or affirmation can help.

"I'm okay without this thing. It would be nice to have it, but if it's not mine to have, I'm still going to be okay." Because you will be.

There's nothing wrong with you. Period. Forever and ever. Amen.

If I Were More (Fill-In-The-Blank) I'd be More (Fill-In-The-Blank).

The easiest way of disproving this most bogus of assumptions is to achieve whatever that *fill-in-the-blank* is. You'll discover you're still not that *fill-in-the-blank*.

So, you finally get the *boyfriend* only to discover he doesn't really *make* you *happy*.

Or you get the *job promotion* and realize once you settle in, you still *want more*.

Another way is to ask someone who has accomplished *fill-in-the-blank* if they're now feeling as if they're more *fill-in-the-blank* because of it.

You have one journey this go around. It's yours. It's not someone else's. They're having theirs. If you were more *successful, or prettier, younger, more famous or popular,* or any of the things you think you need to have more of to get what you want, you'll realize that those delineations are always going to be changing because *you're* always changing.

Since you're always changing—or evolving—the things you

want or identify with, or feel are important to you and help shape you *right now* will not be the same things you will need or even want twenty-five years from now.

Stop filling in your blanks with fictional *fill-in-the-blanks*. Otherwise, when you do fill them in, you'll see they are still empty.

Money. Success. Fame. Marriage. Is The Answer.

To what?

Climate Change?
Death?
Joy?
Worthiness?
Gratitude?
Self-love?
Self-acceptance?

There is no answer in any *thing*. Things help us realize that the answers lie within us.

So it's fine to have money, success, fame, and love. It makes life a little easier with those things than without, I suppose.

But the answer you're seeking can only be found in one place.

If you don't know where that is yet (or by now) you have to keep searching.

I can't tell you the answer. No one can.

Creating is Problem Solving.

Creativity, as we have explored, is both a *result* of past trauma, hardship, and challenges *while you are, at the same time,* converting that raw material *into* your art. That is the *real* process.

Without those experiences you wouldn't be where you are today. Or maybe you'd be a different you. Either way, all steps are necessary on your walk.

Some people learn by doing. Some people learn by studying. Some by doing everything *else* and then realizing they're wasting their time and need to get on to what's most important. Your choices, whatever they are, have also allowed you to build some sort of architecture around the life you're trying to design. All things are valuable.

Every person creating something meaningful is facing her problems. You'll be facing yours.

You're Not At Your Most Creative Constantly Thinking You Have 'Something' To Work On.

This is an old creative narrative we have to change.

It's a myth.

Sure, we have things we need to improve. Sure, we have to develop parts of ourselves and learn. But the simple process of showing up to life is enough. We don't have to add to that by constantly beating ourselves up with self-defeating dialogues that perpetuate the myth—we're lacking, or flawed, or messed up to such a degree that our work isn't perfect.

Life will give you plenty of stuff to look at. Don't worry. That's the nature of living. But if it's not broken why do we assume it must be fixed? It doesn't.

So stop doing that.

You're good enough.

Science proves that we are our best when we're in play. When we *enjoy* what we're doing.

Try that and see how much more "work" you'll get done and it won't even feel like work.

Someone recently asked me, "When my work feels like play, I have a sneaking suspicion that it isn't worth what it 'should' be worth. Why do I feel that when it's fun it isn't really work?"

It *is* work. But the *drama* we associate with it is unnecessary.

Some assembly *is* required. But the suffering is optional.

Sort of like life itself.

Fun doesn't mean insignificance. It means you're really on to something! For if it isn't, why else would you do it?

Do I Have Talent?

Sure you do. Everyone does.

But it's impossible to find when:

A) You're comparing yourself to those who are deemed talented.

And

B) You're trying to be like those people.

Stop emulating. Be yourself.

The people who you admire are doing it their way by having found their way.

You can do that too.

Most people stop before they get really good at something (aka talent), because they underestimate how long it takes.

The point is—just do it.

So the long way is the shortcut.

And remember, talent is your humanity.

Since you're reading this book, you're human. So you're talented.

You Don't Need More Confidence. You Need More Courage.

Author Seth Godin says that and he's right.[6]

You'll do lots of things and feel like you're on top of the world and then do other things and wonder what the heck happened. The goal isn't to become more confident, although certainly doing things over and over again makes you better.

The goal is to become more courageous.

Courage trumps confidence every time. And it's really what's mostly needed every time you do something that's scary and *worth doing*. (Which coincidentally is making art.)

Things worth doing are those things that are new. They are things that ask you to step out of your comfort zone, live in greater risk and uncertainty, give up old ideas of yourself and require you to do them without knowing the outcome.

Feel the fear and do it anyway, and you'll discover that is a lot more reliable and *real* than being confident.

Be Louder.

I once heard a story that blew my mind.

There was a slumber party. A group of ten-year-olds packed in the host's bedroom.

Forts were built, pillow fights ensued, lots of sugary things were consumed, jokes shared, games played, stories told.

Laughter. Screaming. Shouting. Playing.

Not once did the parents supervising the party knock on their kid's door and warn the monsters, "Hey guys! Please make more noise in there!"

Not once.

How many times were we told as rambunctious, wild kids to "keep it down?"

Why have we lost this wild, expressive, joyful, dangerous, adventuresome celebration of life as adults?

Start making noise again.

In your art.

My goals in life have now changed.

I hope someone will knock on my door and remind me to "keep it down in there!"

Purpose.

Everyone seems to be obsessed with "finding their purpose" nowadays.

What if there is none?

(And really, to be able to ask, "What is my purpose?" is a luxury in life that most people on the planet can't even afford.)

But since it's trendy to talk about it these days, let's dig in. We spend so much time wondering and trying to find it, that we miss what's right in front of us.

Your purpose is revealed in each moment that you are yourself. Create from there.

Purposefulness is in the *now*. It is the *intention* from which you engage in whatever it is you're doing. From the most mundane to the most miraculous. And it changes. All the time. If you were doing something else—which you might still do in your long life—there would be (and will be) purpose in that too.

As we move through life, a lot of our "purpose" comes as a result of something we *fall* into.

I think people have mistakenly co-opted the word "purpose", when it really means *to find meaning.*

That's all that it is — a process whereby you are making meaning out of life, which at some level, is meaningless or defies meaning.

And that can be scary to people, so we use words that make us feel safe. If we have "purpose" we can derive *meaning* from a life that is so random and so perilous that to have no purpose would mean oblivion.

But finding our purpose can also have a dark side, inducing shame and unhappiness, comparisons, and competition.

Purpose has nothing to do with what we do. It's not aspirational. It's not tied to doing something. Because you can fail at doing something. Does that mean, if I fail, I've failed at my purpose in life? At one level, if you equate purpose only with successful achievement then, yes, by that standard you will have failed at your purpose. Which is absurd.

If it's something someone can fail at then, is your purpose lost because you don't succeed?

Do kids have purpose? Are babies not important because they lack purpose?

Purpose is something we affix on ourselves to give ourselves value as we grow into adulthood.

My purpose as a child was to play. To exist. To be. Isn't that enough? Do we now have to accomplish something to have more value? (Actually, as a child, I didn't even know there was a purpose to *anything*.)

Meaning is in being. It's not in *what we do*.

Choose Yourself.

The gatekeepers (the corporations or bosses or financiers) get to bestow acknowledgment that we are worthy or talented or the next big thing. They become the de facto tastemakers. I mean, at some level I get it; it's their money. And as we learned earlier, the people with the most money get to make the most calls.

But who made them the gatekeepers in terms of *taste*? Why do they get to decide?

Why is the system set up where someone gets to decide if you are good enough?

You decide and then find a way to get your work—and yourself—out there in some fashion.

"Choose yourself," as author James Altucher likes to call it.[7]

Why are we trying to amass acceptance from the masses who are nameless and faceless to us? And might possibly have *awful* taste?

Don't chase the consent of the easily consensual.

Chase honest work.

Create the thing you wish existed in the world.

Instead of going for the multitudes, what if you made a difference in one person's life? Start there. And it should be your own.

From there, maybe someone else will get it, be inspired by it. So that's two. That's a lot. Two people who really dig what you're doing.

Maybe if you're lucky more people will open their gates and let you in. But you don't need them to.

You don't need permission to *really, truly* affect someone's life. You can simply do it. And that's rare and something worth striving for.

Competition.

There is no competition.

Who do you compete with most in life?

Yourself.

You are your own worst/best competitor. You don't have to "be so good that they can't refuse you", because they will still refuse you even if you are the greatest.

The greatest have been refused and rejected many times, but they kept going.

Our culture is obsessed with the idea of "the best" because it's a way to keep us striving for this mythic ideal that you only matter if you're "#1" or the "Greatest of all time."

Whose time? What is time? For what period? Does it include just the modern age or is the *greatest of all time* inclusive of some 4.5 billion years of existence? (Because if it is, I'd still like to give a shout-out to the G-O-A-T, Mr. Tetrapod.)

Is it just the last 50,000 years when Homo sapiens first developed language or does it stretch back to when the hominid line originated?

Does it include Jesus (Christians would say he's the *greatest!*) or Buddha (He was *so* great!) or during the Greek Ages of Aristotle? How do you quantify the greatest of all time when we weren't alive to understand what time—and the people living during such periods—meant.

A person who is considered "the G.O.A.T." isn't probably thinking of themselves that way. They're not walking around saying, "I'm the greatest." Instead, they're probably doing what all of us are doing. Trying to improve their skills, create new goals and achieve them. Sure they may run faster or jump higher than you or I, but in their minds, they're working on the utilitarian aspect of creating.

They just do it.

Aren't we all great for just being here? We won the lottery just by being incarnated.

How can you be competing against someone else who is completely different from you?

It's subjective.

Let it go. You're never competing against anyone. Except yourself, which is more about putting undue expectations and pressures on yourself to be someone you aren't. Or to beat yourself up by *comparing* yourself to others, which then in your mind *does* make it a competition.

You're already good enough by being who you are. And, in

the subjective-ness in a subjective world, forcing yourself to be "the best" is a zero-sum game. You can't compare something that isn't measurable.

You do it for yourself.

You push yourself to be the best version of you. For you.

If other people get you, that's great. If other people don't, that's okay too. Because you realize throughout the journey of your life, the real person you have wanted the acceptance, love, and adulation from is simply yourself.

Exceptionalism.

You're not exceptional. Get over yourself.

That's such a blow to the ego, but dismantling our own self-importance is one of the biggest breakthroughs to creative freedom. When you realize what you do isn't really that important in the big scheme of things, you're simultaneously freer to create in a way that's less results-oriented, and therefore more dangerous, wild, experimental, and fun.

You, like me, and all the other 7.7 *billion* people on the planet are the same. Average. We simply are human beings fumbling our way through our lives of mystery and uncertainty.

Exceptionalism—thinking that we are more special because of our talents, or looks, or status, or wealth, or rockin' gym body, or whatever the standard our ego uses to define our importance—can interfere with our ability to create. The more we become invested in how important we are, the more we become afraid of taking risks, failing and making mistakes. Or worse, we define our self-worth only through our accomplishments.

The idea of exceptionalism has to do with the things a person does. People certainly have extraordinary talents, skills, and abilities in specific areas. A gifted piano player or an inspiring singer or an incredible athlete all demonstrate their gifts through these endeavors. But it doesn't make them exceptional as a human being. It just makes them great at what they do.

But who are they when they aren't performing these skills? They're normal people. Figuring out their lives, going through a divorce or wanting to adopt a baby or striving to overcome an addiction.

A dentist can be exceptional at fixing your teeth, but horrible at fixing a car. A soccer player can be exceptional at being a goalie but awful in coordinating their outfits. If the person no longer does the thing that makes them exceptional (which, in our capitalist society is often designated by how much money you earn), are they no longer so?

Once again, the distinction lies in our not defining ourselves by what we do.

Exceptionalism is tied to capitalism. It's tied to marketing and advertising and making money off a product by way of a person's achievement. If you're the best or #1, then corporate America will find a way to exploit that into endorsing their cereal or investing in their bank or drinking their cola. The correlation they're trying to make is that *their* product is what made this person exceptional. Or, exceptional people *buy* and *use* their products and if you want to be exceptional, you should too.

Meanwhile, we can drink as much soda as they're trying to sell us and still not hit the ball as great as the "greats" do.

You don't have to aspire to be exceptional. It's fiction. Aspire to be more you. A real, achievable goal.

I love the Emily Dickinson quote that sums up life for all of us, "I'm nobody! Who are you? Are you nobody, too?"[8]

Perfection.

Perfectionism is hiding. (And then lying that we're hiding. And then trying to control our lying *and* hiding.)

"If I can do this thing perfectly then everyone will love me for it," is the mantra of the perfectionist.

And if they love it, I will love myself.

That's where our thinking goes.

If we are trying to do something perfectly, we will never *fully* do the thing. Why? Because the standard of perfection will never allow us to finish it, release it, send it, share it, or publish it. It will never be good enough; it will *never be perfect*. So we hide, lie and control.

Our idea of perfection will keep us from giving the gift to the world because we will always be "perfecting" it before we share it.

If we did the thing, knowing that it wasn't perfect, we would have to take the risk that it might still not work, or we could fail or other people might not like us, or our work.

But that's art.

The perfection principle is a way for us to gather as much control as we can, so we hide the truth—we're scared to make mistakes.

Don't let your need for control keep you from creating and sharing. The longer you try to make something perfect, the longer you'll be hiding yourself from not only the world but the real you. And what a shame that would be.

You're good enough, even, and especially if you've never been told you're good enough.

So much of my life has been spent playing catch up to this fiction that I'm not okay. So if I do *everything* better than okay (i.e., perfect) then eventually I'll be okay.

See how that works?

Except it doesn't.

The problem might be that *you* don't think you're good enough. And no amount of *doing* is ever going to make you good enough.

You have to start with where you are.

You don't have to be the greatest who ever lived. You just have to be good enough. For you.

Voice.

I will listen to that voice *within*

no matter how many times

I have ignored it

and will probably continue to ignore it even though

I know what it tells me is the truth,

and I pretend that I'm not listening

because I'm so distracted by the familiar, loud, negative noise

that takes up so much space,

I mistake it for

the voice.

Time(ing).

If you think about it, most things in life you're capable of doing, you're capable of doing *right now*.

The problem is you think you have time. And are waiting for the perfect timing for things to come together before you start them.

You will wait forever.

Start now. Ask someone out. Go to class. Write a novel. Plant a tree. Move to Canada. Live a less cluttered life. Start meditating. Go to the gym. Reconnect with an old friend.

Timing, then, might also be created by your willingness to take the idea of time *out of it completely* and instead just do it. Now.

So *time* becomes *now*. Which is all there ever will be anyway.

As novelist Doris Lessing says, "Whatever you're meant to do, do it now. The conditions are always impossible."[9]

I Don't Know.

Of course you do.

You say, *"I don't know"* to keep yourself from moving in the direction you want to go, so it's just a form of fear, masked as confusion.

Or because you know the right thing is the hard thing to do, you say, *"I don't know,"* because it buys you time.

The more we say, *"I don't know"* when we do, the longer we prolong our unhappiness, dissatisfaction, and unhealthy situations.

Even when we actually *don't know* something we often vamp about it until

A) we do
or
B) pretend that we do.

Why do you hold yourself in a fog of not knowing about those things within yourself that require you to take the leap?

Because *knowing* is a lot more honest and scary. (Re-read the chapter on *lies.*)

Take the leap. The fog will dissipate, and stuff you didn't think you knew will become very, very clear.

Technique.

The reason we have technique is to transcend it. That's what Yo-Yo Ma says.[10]

He once did an experiment where he played his cello in a New York City subway, and no one recognized the classically trained virtuoso. One of the most revered classical musicians of the last few decades was treated like any other city busker.

Which is to say he was *ignored*.

Technique is to learn how to express the emotion and feeling through the art form you are working in. That's it.

It's the architecture that supports the entire structure.

If you have no understanding or articulation of subtler aspects of feeling, then technique is required.

Technique is sitting down and writing every day.

Technique is going to the gym.

Technique is strapping on your Apple Watch and getting your 10,000 steps a day.

In other words, it's utilitarian to get us to express the profound. (Or sometimes the mundane, too.)

It's the support that allows you to fly.

And you fly by flying your way.

Make Art That Scares You.

We are living in scary times.

We look the same. We sound the same. We all watch the same thing. We buy the same shit. We listen to the same music. We dress the same. We are told which social media apps are cool and hip and *required* to be on. The tech companies know what we like and buy and surf and talk about. So they advertise more of that to make us feel better and keep us in our echo chambers of comfort and sameness.

Our eyes become attuned to the pleasant. Our ears become accustomed to the familiar. We stay in the comfort zone prescribed by society. Just a little bit of provocation or edge to stimulate us out of our somnambulistic state, but not *too much* that might shake us to our core and make us completely rethink our lives and our beliefs.

Zombies we have become. Each of us.

We're being herded by the powers that want us to *not* think. Brainwashed into believing what's hot or fashionable or pretty or sellable or fun.

Until a revolution happens. Or a pandemic. Or a social justice movement. Or all of it.

When I was in grad school in London in the early '90s I somehow got hooked into some of the rad rocker chicks of that period—Alison Moyet, Kim Wilde, PJ Harvey, Lisa Stansfield, and no one more so than Kate Bush.

Before Madonna.
Before Gaga.
Before Florence + The Machine.

Before these artists used music as not just a platform to sing, but as a visceral, transformative, performance-art piece *experience,* there was Ms. Bush.

My college roommate, Fiona, turned me on to her, or rather forced me to confront my fears from my room next door as she blasted Ms. Bush's *Hounds of Love* album.

I hadn't even heard of Kate Bush when I moved to London for a year to get my Master's Degree in Theatre. Fiona would blast Kate's music at all hours of the day, mostly when she was working through her rage and resentment towards her cheating Scottish boyfriend, Colin, who spent most of his time in Glasgow far away from Fiona.

She'd lock herself in her room and crank her tape cassette player to the highest decibel. The whole house reverberated with the strains and sounds of harmony meeting disharmony. Music that wasn't merely music.

It was haunting. It was beautiful. It was scary and weird and edgy and sensual and discordant and made me *very* uncomfortable.

Sort of like Fiona, who sometimes emerged from her room after being holed up for hours looking slightly deranged in her all-black outfits as if she'd just drank five pints of lager and was channeling her own fairy nymph musical seductress, cheeks mascara-streaked from nonstop crying, clothes damp with sweat from her exhaustive interpretive dancing. She'd emerge as if reborn— Kate's penetrating voice pushing Fiona through her personal chrysalis.

I wondered about women as Goddesses and their ability to inhabit different worlds and let themselves be wild in ways I longed to know.

Kate Bush straddled such worlds.

She didn't want us to just listen to a sweet melody that we could hum along to. She didn't want us to succumb to the mind-numbing repetitive beats of pop commercial radio. The sameness of what our ears were accustomed to hearing.

She wanted to make us think. And *feel*. And think some more. And feel more deeply. She wanted to disturb us and shake us out of our dumb little worlds we created for ourselves. (And this was the '90s and not nearly so homogenized as it is now.) She wanted us to not be passive listeners.

She wanted us to realize that we could think for ourselves. That we were also artists. She wanted us to form our own opinions about life and Mother Earth. About sex, and desire, and death, and parents, and the Abyss. About sounds, and what art is, and music, and storytelling, and theatre, and performance.

Uncontainable. Wild. Free. Beyond labels.

Coming from my Midwest upbringing where my idea of music was listening to *Wham's* "Careless Whisper" and Kenny G's saxophone elevator music, Kate Bush was ephemera to me. She was transcendental while at the same time a scarily *real* human being. A banshee with a voice like a songbird. A pagan witch. An artist who made me confront my own limp attempt at making art, too interested in safety than confronting the things that scared me.

Passive and *performative*. That's what I was.

But she… she was the epitome of provocative disturbance. Her cup runneth over and oozed everywhere I didn't want it (or myself) to go.

Just being alive
It can really hurt.
These moments given
Are a gift from time.
Just let us try
To give these moments back
To those we love… [11]

And that, right there is the purpose of art.

To shake us out of our conventional-ness. To activate us into potentials and, at least, to uncover the mysteries we sometimes like to bury and pretend aren't there.

Go All In.

Maybe we don't go all in because we fear that we have nothing to give. That we're tapped out. That the people we give our art to won't like it and they'll want a refund.

So, we hold back, never really knowing, never really feeling what it might be like to give it our all—to get into the crooked corners, the crawlspace, the dark alleys, and hidden cobwebby parts of ourselves—our crunchy human stuff, and let all of that fearlessly explode through the cosmos.

On the canvas. In our lyrics. On the stage. In our hearts and shared outwardly, an intimate revealing of ourselves.

There is this great chasm I'm trying to cross. A chasm that's hollow and empty. Or maybe it was hollowed out and emptied for me, so that I might fill it with all that's good and true. But to get to that place, I have to cross that chasm. Like crossing that mythological River of Styx. That dark, scary place where our shadows take over and drown us in the Underworld. Sometimes it feels easier *not* to go there, though. The *potential* of who I am and who I know myself to be feels so much *harder* than just being this guy who maybe let the real good stuff slip away.

Everyone contends with this. Partly because it's hard to acknowledge that hidden part of ourselves, the part that safeguards and simultaneously robs us of our human, fallible self. If I can protect myself, it won't hurt quite as much if I get rejected.

Except it does, and you've made it even worse because you held yourself back from the *real* offering. Which is you.

We are often better at *appearing* a certain way than actually being.

Let's go all in by being *all* of who we are. People may still not get it or even like it, but we will become freer by putting ourselves at the center of our work, knowing it's not really about someone liking us anyway. It's about telling our truth and sharing that with the world.

You're Not Here To Entertain People. You're Here To Change People.

A byproduct of creating *might be* to entertain people.

But that's not the reason we create.

We make things because we are fundamentally changed in the process itself and want to take that cathartic aspect of connection out into the world so that our work connects with more and more people, changes people, and gets them to think about themselves and the human condition in a different way.

You have the power to do that.

That's epic. And changes people. And when we change, we are also helped.

So maybe the real reason we are here is to help people.

Re-Think Why You're Creating.

Why do we do stuff? Sometimes, unconsciously, it might be to prove our parents wrong, to get back at someone, to escape, to find love or acceptance, to get rich or famous, to rebuild our self-esteem, or to work out our issues.

If those reasons sustain you, so be it.

I have found, as you continue on an artistic journey, the *real* reasons for doing something become the only things that get you through.

Quitting isn't the bad word our culture makes it out to be. In fact, quitting might give way to new beginnings. New ideas. Different creative paths. Maybe it's more about quitting the *reasons* we do something because we have outgrown those things that no longer nourish or inspire us, or fit where we are heading. They no longer compliment the life we wish to build.

There is nothing in the *Rules of Life* handbook that says you must do the same thing your entire life. You can do many things. Does that make you a "quitter" just because your interest has changed? I used to love roller skating as a kid. Then I outgrew it. Does that make me a quitter?

Maybe something you can't even imagine yet that makes you feel alive in a way you've never experienced is waiting for you later in life. And it can only reveal itself through the processes you are now engaged in. It's all necessary.

Quitting is actually a reset. It's restarting. It's beginning something from a place that truly matters. From a new vantage point that helps you form an essentialness to what you are doing. And that is, forging a different understanding of *yourself.* Meeting yourself head-on in the work you choose to do that asks you to engage mindfully, face your fears, tell your truth and confront the lies you've been told.

That, then, isn't quitting. It's—perhaps for the first time— truly doing it for yourself.

Over Share.

Artistic Rule of Thumb: If you're feeling something while creating, chances are other people will as well.

Use your art to express these variant points of self. Don't censor. Don't inhibit. Use your art to work through the things you fear or feel vulnerable about or have had breakthroughs in.

When I think about the stories that have inspired me the most, whether a book or a play or a musical or film, it's almost always been because the writer or creator over-shared.

I used to watch things and be like, "Oh no she didn't!"

And yes, she did.

The sheer *audacity* of sharing things about oneself so that a taboo is broken.

So that the shame is erased.

So that we can feel that we're not alone with our freakishness and disturbed selves.

Over-sharing is a word that people use who like to keep their lives private and feel threatened by people who tell the truth.

For most people, simply *sharing* is a burden. It's almost too scary to do.

Why do we carry such shame around the things we've survived? Why such shame around the things that have made us who we are? Why are we ashamed when we reveal ourselves to help someone else who's in a situation like our own?

That's not over-sharing. That's storytelling.

One person's over-share is another person's lifeline. Another person's decision to not commit suicide that day. Another person's decision to pursue their dreams.

Your share can literally *save a life*.

Stop trying to present the perfect picture. We've seen enough of those. We want to see the picture of the person *before they pose* to take the picture.

You'll discover that it's not *over* sharing at all.

It's just sharing.

Fame Game.

For decades, when researchers asked kids what they wanted to be when they grew up, the answers were often the same. A mixed bag of "doctor", "astronaut", "teacher", etc. Today, when kids in America are asked the same question—their response—"more than any other occupation on earth, is to be a famous influencer".[12]

Are you still breathing? God Save America.

Fame isn't a goal. It's a byproduct of what we do in a world that, for some reason, turns people into celebrities.

Why?

Fame gives us entry to a world that if we had access to we'd finally be happy.

I don't know if that's what people really believe, but that's certainly what the media likes to portray. And we've all drunk the Kool-Aid.

Social media has driven the frenzy around being relevant (i.e., famous) more than any other platform in this modern age.

We're obsessed with celebrity because the mythology is built into us as a species. We are a culture derived from storytelling. *All culture* comes from stories. Since the ancient Greeks and onwards, civilizations have survived, I think, mostly by storytelling. (And in today's culture I'm convinced that celebrity has replaced the mythic tradition of heroes born out of mythology since culturally, we aren't really connected to any sort of mythic storytelling.)

A lot of storytelling passed down through cultures and generations includes epic battles fought by heroes. These heroes are imbued with superhuman strength. Or agility. Or power.

We, as mere mortals, wanted to be like them, so we prayed to them to invoke our own heroes. Never mind that some of those heroes were monsters.

Then and now.

In Greek Mythology alone, there were so many terrible creatures you can't keep track.

Sisyphus, in between rolling that boulder up a hill, liked to murder his guests.

Tantalus, what a hoot he was. He had a party, killed his son, cooked him and fed him to his guests.

Medea—don't invite her to your wedding, please! She gave her previous husband's new bride a dress that burst into flame when she wore it and then she murdered all of her own kids.

And let's not forget Zeus. The Big Daddy of them all. He constantly cheated on his wife, Hera, and chained poor Prometheus to a rock and had an eagle peck out his liver.

For eternity.

And these were people we aspired to be like? These were Gods we worshipped? These were *heroes?*

We need to rethink our priorities.

We don't consider who people are *behind* the masks. Maybe that's because we are blinded by the brightness of their eleven million social media followers, or their 8-pack abs, or perfect house, or their dazzling photos taken from all over the world. Or maybe we just like to hold on to the *fantasy* of a thing. It's sexier than reality.

But they're just people. Like you and me.

They can be selfish and unkind. Gossipy and prejudiced. Kind and considerate and intolerable and small-minded.

But fame conceals those qualities because of the luster shining from the star of it all.

Stay connected to the reasons for creating that *are* sustainable.

Joy. Making a difference. Passion. Relationship. Making great friends. Conquering your fears. Making art.

As you get older, the *only* sustainable aspect about creating is doing things with people you love on things you love, anyway.

To be artistic isn't an end goal. Making something—creating a product isn't the end. It's not even really the best part. That's what a commodity-based, money-driven obsessed culture forces us into thinking (and doing). The purpose of art is not the product. It's the process. It's to make people feel and think (hopefully differently) about something *through* the art.

Art is not a noun; art is a verb.

Looking For Answers? It's In Ascension.

Look up.

Novelist Anne Lamott in her *Ted Talk* tells a story about how bees trapped in a mason jar without a lid often can't find their way out.[13] They're all bumping around at the bottom of the jar. Why? Because they don't simply look up and fly away.

How do we stop getting stuck in the mason jars of our lives?

Ascension.

Sure we can look elsewhere for quick fixes and distractions and things that make us feel better in the short-term. But long-term insight and breakthroughs occur by shifting our awareness to a completely different domain.

So we have to look somewhere else. Upwards is as good of a place to look as any other. And if we think of consciousness as something that is part of awareness or universal mind, it simply isn't found just *here* in the physical reality of what we're looking at. It involves tuning into things that you actually *can't see*.

Ms. Lamott says it's about simply looking up. And that's one way. But it's often about throwing our entire body and soul and heart and guts into that act. Really *feeling* our way to a higher place. What that place might be, is different for each of us. Or maybe it's all things, or maybe it changes all the time.

It could be God one day, and on Wednesdays it's the sky. It could be a prayer in the morning and in the afternoon a bowl of warm soup. It could be singing a song. It could be watching the clouds go by or daydreaming.

Ascension for someone else might be found in nature or watching airplanes, listening to a bird's song or swimming in the ocean. Find your transcendental place. Go there. Find the place that elevates your eyes, and heart, and hope to a higher level. It can be taking a walk or making bread. It's different for everyone.

It is almost always, also, found in forgiveness. Forgiving ourselves for all the shitty things we do and forgiving others for the shitty things they do too.

It can be a smile or just breathing *into* your heart.

The answers really come. They do. From *someplace else* that is then experienced in the here-and-now.

Look up! Look up! There is always a way. Just look up, look up dear friend.

The Porn Problem.

Our world is quickly becoming a digital porn wasteland. There's Food Porn, TV Porn, Phone Porn. Instagram Porn, Youtube Porn, Sports Porn, Social Media Porn, Car Porn. Oh, and regular Porn Porn. News Porn, Fashion Porn, Music Porn, Video Game Porn, Gossip Porn, Shopping Porn, Gadgets Porn, Netflix Porn.

Basically, we are products of and have given birth to Porn Culture. A culture of addiction. A culture that's so brilliant at distracting us into consuming and becoming automatons that we are losing connection to things that are real. Actually *things* aren't real at all. That's the problem. We've lost connection to ourselves and to others.

Now some addictions are socially acceptable. Some not.

Pick your poison: wine, cigarettes, pot, partying, shopping, gaming, people, trips. Or not just things, also states of being— the "falling in love" phase, romance, negativity, complaining, being a whiner, victimhood.

Oh, and feelings—anger, sadness, jealousy, rage, resentment.

Anything that works for us in the short term by anesthetizing us and making us feel good (while at the same time making us feel bad, and preventing us from feeling *other* feelings) is what I would consider porn.

Obviously, socially acceptable addictions to the kinds mentioned above aren't considered addictions. They're funny or neurotic or party-acceptable. But tell someone you're a heroin, crystal meth or gambling addict, and you are immediately demonized. *That's the bad stuff.*

But it's fine if you're constantly on Instagram; checking out, disconnected, depressed and anxious. It's encouraged that you binge-watch a hundred different shows on Netflix. Or you're on TikTok more than you are with yourself. Or your family.

The problem with socially acceptable forms of being a serotonin junkie is that eventually the porn ends. The bottle drains empty. You run out of cigarettes. You can only troll on social media for so long. You get tired of the same porn actors. There's only so many times you can watch a penis do its thing.

Then what? You breathe and realize you're empty. Or not empty but lonely. Or not lonely but separate and alone. Bored. Scared. Unsure what to do. So, we fill ourselves up again with some other form of distraction and numbing cream and start another day.

Addictions, for many of us, substitute for an emptiness we feel in our lives—or boredom, or fear—as it momentarily attempts to fill this void or mask scary emotions.

We have completely forgotten that life is *supposed* to be mundane, at times. Instead of dwelling in spaces of contemplation and yes, even boredom, we've been driven to distract our-selves out of *being.*

Gary Zukav says, "When you strive to heal an addiction, you're reaching for your highest goal. So it is profoundly spiritual."[14]

As we have been discovering in this book, somewhere em-bedded in the problem is also the solution. But you have to want the solution more than the problem, which on the sur-face seems easy. The truth is, addiction to anything is also an addiction to a problem.

But whenever you come down from any high, the realization hits. What are you left with?

Yourself in this body.
Figuring your shit out.
Questioning why you are here.

Escapism is just that. An opportunity to forget that you are mortal and very limited.

My therapist once told me, "Even the princess poops."

And that right there gets to the core of the porn problem—refusing to admit that even the perfect princess poops. Porn in all forms presents an unreal package of something—like most things that are commercialized and sold to us wrapped in a beautiful red bow. If you never get beyond the package—no pun intended—you never have to deal with all the stuff that's *inside* the package. Like poop. The things that can't be covered up continuously with sparkle or air freshener. (Insta-gram surely has a filter for that.)

But that's where the intimacy is. And that's scary. The distraction seems so much better because if I'm distracted, I don't really have to move forward with confronting the porn that's distracting me from what I need to face.

Maybe what has happened is that we have become so programmed by the tiny dopamine rewards—the dings and bells and alerts and whistles and likes and hearts and shares— that we have inebriated ourselves with tiny micro-climaxes all day long. Just one more follower and *Bam!* Nirvana.

What the software companies are hoping is that we get so hooked into that gratification-impulse-feedback loop that we lose connection to the real *climax* we seek in life. The spark that ignited the entire universe. Gave birth to the stars. Molded planets. Created constellations. It was one gigantic fuck. One huge cosmic orgasm that came without judgment or shame or regret or fear of contracting an STD.

I want to have more of those interstellar moments. With my lover and with friends, sharing cosmic ideas and creative inspirations. With myself in deep meditation and talking about things that inspire and stay with us.

And ultimately, more profoundly with myself.

You are your own highest high you will ever encounter. More than any other experience in life, discovering oneself is the high we're all searching for. Ironic that we spend it so long searching everywhere else through everyone else. It takes a badass to not fall victim to the idea that "my other half" will make me whole. Your other half is inside you. He or she exists within. The inner self with the outer self completes wholeness. God incarnated inside *and* out.

Indian philosophy says that God so wanted to experience himself as God that he cut himself in two as a human being so that the observer can observe the Divine through the Divine's eyes without realizing he or she *is* the Divine.

So that's why you, just plain old you, are the highest high you'll ever know, and maybe also why we can never know anyone else. Fully. We're all expressions of the Divine wanting to know more deeply ourselves through our experiences here that bring us finally back to self.

And embracing that. Uncovering yourself and realizing that higher *You* loves you just as you are—your fears and shame and fucked-up-ness and beauty and addictions and disconnects and porn problem.

And *that* is the biggest, most beautiful cosmic fuck you're ever going to experience.

Safari As Metaphor For Life.

I was on safari in South Africa years ago and the guide, Headman, started telling me how he went through a period in his life questioning what he was doing. His life dream was to lead safaris and educate people about wildlife preservation and then he started listening to others.

Which meant doubting himself.

By listening to parents. "Experts." Well-meaning friends. Exes.

"You should be married by now." "You should have a girlfriend." "Why don't you make more money?" "What can this lead to?" "When are you going to grow up and get a real job?" "You're missing out on the good life."

Headman began to question everything. He began to wonder if he made a mistake. The thing he loved doing—observing animals in their natural habitat—became old hat to him. He grew bored and lost his sense of wonder. He would robotically drive visitors into the bush yawning, "Oh, there's a rhino." (As if seeing a rare rhino was like seeing an ordinary dairy cow.)

A tremendous amount of soul-searching occurred. He stopped listening to people who wanted what was best (and more convenient) for them (but not for him), and he slowly regained his passion for what he wanted to do.

"Look! Holy Shit! There's a rhino! How amazing is that?"

The lesson learned is to not allow ourselves to be contaminated by drops of poison that people (sometimes even well-meaning ones) seem to want us to ingest.

Headman said he had to start "seeing things anew and return to planting flowers and appreciating the beauty in it all."

Safari is a metaphor for life.

Get out there. Seek the experience. Stay out of the end results. Go on the adventure. Commune with nature. Spend time with animals who teach us presence and living in the moment. Trust your heart. Listen to people who support what it is you want for yourself.

And mostly, do it for yourself and be in a wonderful f*ck it.

That's safari. That's life.

How To Recover From Door Slams.

A bird flew into the window of my house the other day. I was sitting in the living room, working, and all of a sudden I heard this tremendous thud against the pane of the glass windowed doors. I went outside and there was this little bird on his back, totally stunned, as if in some sort of coma, but alive. I wanted to find out what kind of bird it was, but gave up after an extensive round of googling and decided to just name him Charlie.

I went to get some kitchen gloves (Avian flu is no joke!) and when I ran back to tend to him I found he had flipped himself over. Charlie was gathering his wits about him, I think, clearing out the cobwebs from his collision.

We hung out like that for the longest time. Me lying down next to him, observing him and his dinosaur-like features. He, eyeing me but seemingly relaxed (or possibly still simply in shock). Finally, after enough time had passed, Charlie got up and flew away. Just like that.

No harm, no foul. Pun intended.

There's a meaning to everything, I thought as I watched him

take flight and disappear into the trees as quickly as he had arrived unexpectedly on my balcony.

In life, and in your career, you're going to hit a wall. Or get a door slammed in your face. Honestly, the better you're doing, the more doors are likely to hit you; it's a reflection of you putting yourself out there.

What we need to do, like this little bird, is learn not to take failure personally. Charlie didn't. Charlie wasn't sitting around saying, "Who put that door in my way?" He just took the time necessary to regroup and go back to doing what he was made to do: fly.

We aren't entitled to anything. Doors are everywhere. A few might open, most will not. You're going to get hit, figuratively and sometimes literally. It's going to happen. It's life.

So we can't take it personally when we encounter setbacks, even when they are painful, jarring, and disorienting. At a certain point, everybody experiences door slams in their life. The idea that once you get the thing you always wanted, it's all going to be easier, is an illusion. The doors *still* shut but now they might be a bit more decorated, elaborate, and *expensive*. Get my drift?

These door slams are part of what make you who you are. When you acknowledge that those moments are part of the bigger picture, you free yourself from anger and resentment, and you can get back on track that much faster. And once that happens, like Charlie, you'll fly.

Who Are You?

That might be the best question to keep asking yourself daily. You'll realize who you are is more a revelation of what and who you are not.

If you don't know who you are then how can you make art?

Art requires a very personal point-of-view. And often, a life-or-death commitment to tell a story, or fight for a cause, or make a decision to overcome huge obstacles to share your work with the world. Without knowing who you are, what you stand for, what you believe in, and what you wish to say through your personal self-expression, you become a spectator of your own life. Unseen. Unspecific.

Don't worry so much if you haven't figured it out yet. Or that your opinions and passions might be wrong. Have them anyway. They might change as you move along your journey. Hopefully they will. By exercising your viewpoints about things, you move forward in the world, articulating a more present, passionate, and capable you.

And with more you, comes so many more powerful things, including your art.

Ex Nihilo.

We all begin with a blank slate. Nothing. Zip. Nada. Tabula rasa. The void. A white canvas. An empty page. A bare stage.

So if you're facing that image in whatever form it might take—cans of colored paints, a pair of dancing shoes, an opened acting class page on your computer's browser—you've already gotten to the first impasse.

Now jump.

You have to hit the buzzer before you know the answer. If you wait, chances are you won't act on any impulse, idea or well-meaning intention.

If you signed up for a class, or put down a deposit, or you went and bought a new keyboard—that's the jumping off point. Good for you! You're doing more than most people do in their lifetimes.

Once you jump over the hurdle and into the real game of life, what you're going to contend with, though, is much, much harder than perhaps the act itself.

The demons or *lies* that rattle around in our heads. (But let us also always remember that without the demons we wouldn't really know an angel if it flew right up to us).

Or... since I'm on this angel metaphor for a hot minute—isn't a demon just an angel in a different disguise?

Now back to our regularly scheduled point here since I got distracted by the celestial realms. For our purposes, we are confronting those demons that sometimes get louder the closer we get to our goal—admonishing us, warning us, scaring us into believing something isn't meant for us.

Or maybe this tiny thing here *is* meant for you. But to want more is taboo. That's not for you. That's reserved for someone else.

The Greats.
The *VIPs*
The Influencers.
The Popular Ones.

Why are we trying to be popular?

Life is Groundhog's Day of revisiting high school repeatedly but with grayer hair, wrinkles, expanded waistlines, and more pathetic attempts to be relevant in a world swimming with irrelevance and meaninglessness, perpetrated by the greatest swindlers ever assembled—the Tech Companies. Their "social" platforms— engineered by *Bots* and algorithms—make us feel inadequate because we are comparing ourselves to the unreal.

But we can graduate from this purgatory (Yeehaw!) of trying to please, be cool, and part of the "in" crowd. We don't have to be bullied by those people we mistakenly considered the insiders—the people we longed to be. If we're lucky, we'll discover that the outsiders are the interesting ones, and the margins are where all the creative, dangerous, wild, brilliant ones hang out.

That's where, truly, all the cool people are.

The demons *and* the angels.

And that's where you want to stay.

Be A Beauty Enhancer.

Political activist Savanna Madamombe left Zimbabwe in 2000 during the regime of the corrupt President Robert Mugabe. From her new life in Manhattan, she saw how her beloved home fell apart so she organized protests denouncing him, started chat groups, and became a vocal critic of his regime. Since it was unsafe for her to go back to her country, she had to wait 18 years until he was ousted from power in 2017.

She returned to the capital and immediately started pointing out how the city had deteriorated and fallen into disarray. She held councilmen accountable for their refusal to clean up the city. She encouraged citizens to do the same. Since Mugabe's removal from office, she has moved back to her country to make Zimbabwe beautiful again.

She and her team, wearing *Fix Zimbabwe Or Die Trying* t-shirts, set out to re-garden all the plant boxes among one of the city's main thoroughfares with flowers.

In most cities, this would not be revolutionary. In Harare, it was unheard of. Any form of protest, however small, could elicit a violent response from authorities under Mugabe. Even planting flowers in a public space.

"Forget the flowers," Madamombe says, "It's a symbol. I'm hoping this will start a conversation. That's essential. That has been gone for a long time."[15]

She's a beauty enhancer.

So am I. So are you. So is everyone on the planet.

Enhance the beauty with your work.

We are the only species (that we know of) who make things with meaning and care for *the sake of beauty*. We make things for the sheer joy of making them. It's in our DNA. We make things we don't need and some people don't even want (!) just so we can carve out a little more beauty in this place that is already beautiful.

Let's put our attention on that. It might be idyllic. But it gives us greater motivation to beautify little corners of our lives. First, beautify our thoughts and actions, then the areas where we live and work. And it will ripple out to our community and our cities and towns. Before you know it, huge transformation can occur everywhere.

Like all things, start small. And you'll see that yes, even *you* are making a difference, in the simplest yet most profound ways.

Finish Your Un-Finished Business Of Childhood.

I heard that statement recently. It's provocative. And true, in theory. We don't want to let our unconscious, unaware parts of ourselves sabotage our lives.

But at some level, even if you do "finish" it—it's never done. And maybe it's not supposed to be.

All that stuff of childhood, the pain and *awfulness*—All. Of. It.—is essential.

It's not something to be finished. It's something to heal. To understand, to love and accept, and forgive.

Carry it along with you. Because you are anyway. You can't just exorcize a part of yourself. You can't just trash it and be done with it forever. You can learn to live with it and accept it but you can't remove it from you. You can't cut it out from your heart, or kidney or spleen. The adult who survived and your inner child who sustained the brunt of the injuries has been with you since you began the journey.

And isn't that beautiful? She's not forsaken you even though you have abused her and rejected her and made fun of her and railed against her—maybe similarly to what happened to you *when* you were a kid. We blame that child as if the child should have known (or done) better.

Instead of perpetuating the cycle of abuse, let's try something else.

Invite her in. Let her sit on the couch with you. Let her share in your laughs and pain. Let her awaken inside you again and show you what you're not addressing. Let her show you what she came here to teach you.

Because there is certainly something to learn. To not listen, to not accept our past and incorporate the wisdom one gains in having experienced it, is the real unfinished business. The real heartache.

For there is truly nothing more tragic than being an adult separated from our own child. That is the real trauma that we keep revisiting.

Your Kryptonite Is Also Your Superpower.

It's all connected.

The part we want to remove from ourselves is the very part we need to transcend or transform into something that powerfully works for us.

As the *Odyssey* and other great metaphorical stories tell us, the adventure—the leaving *home* is what eventually takes us back there. But first, you have to go on the adventure. And that simply means be willing to let go of the known. Risk the not knowing. Risk the new and uncomfortable, the foreign.

The thing that scares you about yourself is the very thing you must call forth to arrive at a new you. You don't get there by denying it, or avoiding it. You use it, or it uses you. That's what the journey is about.

We think it's about making a piece of art in some form or fashion. Which—at the external level—it is. But that's a metaphor for what you have to confront in yourself.

Our creative expressions mirror where we are, what we fear,

what makes us feel vulnerable, and what we're trying to overcome.

That's what art is.

To Be An 'Amateur' Is To Be A Lover Of Something.

The Old French meaning of "Amateur" was to be a *lover of something*.[16]

How did that get translated through the ages to mean not proficient, less-than, unprofessional or second-rate?

According to that definition, if you're an amateur, you suck.

A professional is a label for someone who gets paid for her occupation, regardless of skill level. An amateur, not so much.

So you're considered a hobbyist.

There are an awful lot of brilliant, skilled, geniuses in all kinds of fields who aren't even recognized as "professional." Culture hasn't labeled them as anything but amateur.

Be an amateur! I beg you! Be a lover of things. Invest in things with your whole heart and soul.

I'd rather be an amateur with an open heart and lots of misses than a professional without integrity or passion attached to his hits.

As amateurs we make things. Creating art is different than *selling* art.

If you only consider yourself a professional once you have sold something, you've sadly probably never met your true, amateur self. And to create art without love is ultimately not art at all.

Time. Part Two.

Business Insider (of all places!) recently printed a list of accomplished artists in all fields who were considered "late bloomers"[17].

It's a great reminder that whoever you are, wherever you are, you are *exactly* where you need to be. Here are just a few of the accomplishments of some creators who didn't hit their stride until later in life.

Vera Wang didn't begin her career as a designer until she was 40.

Stan Lee created his first hit comic *The Fantastic 4* just shy of his 39th birthday.

Charles Darwin didn't publish *On the Origin of Species* until he was 50.

Samuel Jackson's first lead role was at 43 in Spike Lee's *Jungle Fever*.

Julia Child wrote her first cookbook at 50.

Frank McCourt published his first book, *Angela's Ashes,* at 65, and won the Pulitzer at 78.

You're doing just fine.

When you put a clock on things, you stop enjoying and celebrating your journey, the process of maturing into who you are, and get caught up in creativity being a race.

It's not a race.

You panic that you haven't "made it" based on outside considerations and, as we have explored throughout this book, who made up these external markers of "making it" anyway?

Let's throw them out and start afresh. Work with your own inner pace and your own inner discoveries that deliver you to new places exactly as they should. You decide what works for you. What makes you feel good, what helps you realize that things are unfolding as they should.

Everyone is on their own timeline. As hard as that can be to truly *live,* the more we can breathe into each moment of that acceptance, the more joyful it will be to know it and get to wherever it is that *you* decide you want to go.

Methods.

There are so many "methods" to things. How to paint, write, sing, act, dance, cook, have sex, wash your clothes.

Do we ever wonder *where* and *when* these methods arose?

Maybe some of these methods were devised during the time the person was living in. Maybe a person was facing certain challenges and discovered a way that worked for *her*. At that time.

Don't try to replicate other people's methods.

That's their way. You find your way.

The problem with following other people's methods is that it may not work for you in the short term, and you will give up and find another method, leaving you always searching rather than developing *your own*.

Every person who's walked this incredible walk on this beautiful, lonely planet has made it up as they walked it. (Even when they think they're applying someone else's method.)

Tennis star Serena Williams's longtime coach, Patrick Mouratoglou says this, "My philosophy is I know nothing. I learn the person and I learn my player. A lot of coaches start with their method. [But] there is [only] one method per player and I need to find it."[18]

Each person has his or her own method.

Be braver. Find (and cultivate) yours.

Bigger Isn't Better.

Bigger isn't the point. More isn't the point.

Doing the things you love is. It's not even about acting, or writing poetry, or gardening or writing a novel.

It's about the process—the discoveries and breakthroughs one achieves—while engaging in these acts.

America wants everything to be *big*. We are living in the biggest oversized country in the world. *More* makes us happy. *More* is what we should be going after. *Bigger* is best. *Bigger* illustrates success, or wealth, or power.

How is bigger better if the emptiness of who we are makes everything else not enough?

Oh, I know… Just keep getting more stuff. *Bigger* stuff.

That's the message we are told.

Instead, strive to fill yourself with a fullness of the experiences of being alive. Not with things.

Eventually, you might start to feel a compulsion to get rid of things. Those things that used to be the antidote for filling up what was empty in your life and are no longer needed might end up in the discard pile. Enabling you to get lighter and freer and more full with the things that truly matter. The fullness of being alive.

Silencing The Critic.

The chief critic is the one inside your head.

Silence him. Ignore her. Especially in terms of unfounded, inaccurate and limited assessments of your work, mostly based on past experiences.

When the outside world criticizes you, try to remember:

Criticism has nothing to do with you personally. It's critical about something you made *only* to make it perhaps better.

Don't conflate notes for improvement as attacks against yourself or your talent.

You will do things that are great.

You will do things that aren't so great.

That doesn't have anything to do with you. Or when it does... it doesn't render your work talentless. It just means *this particular thing* perhaps didn't work.

For one person. Or maybe many.

Everyone has an opinion. Everyone's understanding of something they watch, listen to, digest, read, absorb and experience is purely subjective. The subjectivity comes from each person's desires, fears, hates, prejudices, and interests. Don't try to appeal to everyone's tastes. It's impossible and will leave you constantly bullied by your inner critic regaling you as unpopular, non-commercial, or uninteresting.

Remember, in the end, if it worked for *you* that's all that really matters.

Create For Self. Not For Culture.

We create for ourselves. That's not a selfish act, but an act of service.

Why? Because the impulse, the creative genesis comes from a place that inspires us to create the thing that is imagined. It comes *through you and for you.* So it's unique *to you.*

When we do that, we simultaneously create for others. Because the personal also is the universal. So we end up creating, as a byproduct, for our friends, our family, our community, and thereby, culture.

But even though we create for ourselves (and thereby for culture), we don't have to take our cues *from* culture.

That's dangerous. That's also insanity. Culture consumes. It doesn't generate. It mimics; it doesn't originate.

To hold on to your artistic integrity means to create the things you wish to see in the world. If you took your cues from culture you wouldn't follow your unique, original voice. You would try to match what culture has already done. You would try to be accepted or liked or popular. You would try to replicate or reproduce what has worked before. You would try to fit in and be part of the masses. And recreate what you *think* culture wants.

Don't do that.

Culture doesn't know what it wants. That's why it's insatiable and impossible to predict. It's fickle and oftentimes, base and cruel and mean.

Create the thing that can only come through you; it's your gift. It's spirit. It's upliftment. It's revolutionary.

Culture may get it or not. When they do get it, they'll praise it and then try to commodify it, duplicate it, and ask you to make more of the same. And on and on it goes.

Be willing to create independent of what culture is trying to dictate. That's the bravest kind of art we are all called to make.

Journey > Destination.

Imagine there was never a concept called *destination*. Nowhere to end up. No ultimate finale. No final result or ending.

Thrilling, isn't it?

Thousands of years ago, there were no google maps to say, "You have arrived at your destination." The world was unexplored, so vast, so limitless, one could have journeyed thousands of miles and still never come to any ending; never arriving at a destination.

This made me think a lot about the past. Not necessarily *my* past ... but the distant, ancient past. The past of great stories and myth.

The past we only understand through archaeology and anthropology. From the studying of ancient cultures and traditions.

That past.

I read a book this year that explores a new framework for

understanding our Neanderthal cousins (who we owe great gratitude for being here, both genetically and evolutionarily), and how so often we put a contemporary narrative on something that is much, much more complex.

Far from being the brutish, primal creatures our history books like to promulgate, the Neanderthal was decidedly much more like you and I.

Reading a book of such magnitude helped me uncover a greater, more *truthful* perspective of what we each might be grappling with and struggling against during this time. Uncertainty. Fear. Having our life's plans completely disrupted. And it helped me to contextualize how we perhaps have lost sight of our way.

That *The Way* is a living, breathing thing.

The Way isn't a destination point. It's the journey itself.

We have heard many times in our quotable culture that *the journey is the destination.*

But it's more than that.

The truth is there is no arrival. No destination. No homecoming. No ultimate achievement. No finish line.

Our Neanderthal cousins could not conceptualize a destination, because all they did was travel. In part to survive. As hunter-gatherers, they followed *patterns* to sustain them. Those of food, seasons, animal migration and the awareness of life's constantly altering landscape. They traveled as life itself travels.

There is only journeying.

For each of us, and for everyone who came before us.

For you and me, the people we love, the people we fight against, the planet and all its inhabitants; from tribes and peoples and cultures of the past to your neighbor and lover and best friends; your kids and parents.

In a transient world that has its evolutionary beginnings born out of nomadism—it illustrates how the journeying is in our DNA.

In Taoist terms this spiritually could be called *Chi*. The life force that *moves* everything.

Passages.

When I look at society as a whole, I sometimes despair that we have lost our way. Fundamentally. Irretrievably. Disconnected from the rhythm of nature.

But then I take a deep breath and understand that although we are all *journeying together*, it's never been about anyone other than yourself. We decide for ourselves how we want to view the world and ourselves. How we want to move our Chi. How we want to be more conscious of the very-real life force that moves us all along on The Big Journey.

We decide if we want to make our travels one of grievances and complaints or one that celebrates the gift of simply being alive.

———

A pandemic can make you take stock in what you have and what you have squandered. What has been lost and what wasn't even attempted. It puts things in perspective in terms of how much time we have (left) and what we really want to do with it. It makes us lose this sense of "certainty" about life and can therefore break us open into the wonderful capacity we all have to create and share and love *now*.

Uncertainty is scary for most of us. But when you look at our ancient cousins that is *all* they were sure about.

Imagine that.

To be so attuned to the vicissitudes and transitoriness of life, that *uncertainty* wasn't probably a concept.

It just was.

Obviously, modern culture and all its trappings and conveniences have disconnected us from that salient and powerful way to live. To be. And to know.

So maybe Covid has taught us, finally, we're not in charge and we're all part of the mysterious flow, and that all of life is uncertain. *Always.*

You might wonder, how can one, then, be an artist during a time in which art almost feels like an extravagance?

Yet this is *exactly* when we need it. Out of the uncertainty of the Great Plague came the Renaissance. Out of these challenging times a new you is being forged even if you feel nothing has changed yet in your life; except you're getting restless and bored, have gained the dreaded Covid-15 lbs., and are losing your mind watching yet another Netflix series or Tik-Tok video.

Perhaps this subtle awareness that you are a wanderer is the gift that Covid has shown us.

The journeyman-and woman. Journeyers. That's who we are.

What a wonderful, weird, wild, scary, grateful, beautiful time to be alive. As it has *always* been, except we have often forgotten.

Someday anthropologists may discover our history, write about us, explore our ruins and marvel at how adaptable and creative we were during such challenging times.

I hope so. What a gift to leave for future generations of journeyers.

You and I were here. We lived in uncertainty. We embraced its teachings and learned from its truth.

We. Were. Here.

We continue the journey. Bravely. With perhaps a little less burden, a little less heaviness that this past year has taught us to cast aside. It isn't needed on our travels.

Keep journeying. And remain who you have always been.

A Nomad. Searching for truth.

WORKS CITED

1. Waxman, O. B. (2019, July 15). The history of Neil Armstrong's one small step for man quote. Time. Retrieved November 24, 2021, from https://time.com/5621999/neil-armstrong-quote/.

2. Grotowski, J. (1968). Towards a poor theatre. Odin Teatrets Forlag.

3. Charity, Tom. (2001). John Cassavetes: lifeworks. Omnibus Press.

4. Hebrews King James Version 11:1. (2021). Online. http://kingjamesbibleonline.org/Hebrews-11-1/

5. Merriam-Webster. (n.d.). Faith definition & meaning. Merriam-Webster. Retrieved November 24, 2021, from https://www.merriam-webster.com/dictionary/faith.

6. Godin, Seth. Retrieved from Akimbo: A Podcast from Seth Godin. February 14, 2018.

7. Altucher, J. (2013). Choose yourself: Be happy, make millions, live the dream. James Altucher.

8. Academy of American Poets. (n.d.). I'm nobody! who are you? (260) by Emily Dickinson - poems | academy of American poets. Poets.org. Retrieved November 24, 2021, from https://poets.org/poem/im-nobody-who-are-you-260.

9. Lessing, D. (2019). The Golden Notebook. 4th Estate.

10. NPR. (2018, August 17). Yo-Yo Ma, a life led with Bach. NPR. Retrieved November 24, 2021, from https://www.npr.org/transcripts/639571356.1

11. Bush, K 1993. Moments of Pleasure [Song]. On the Red Shoes. Columbia Records.

12. HBO. (2021). Fake Famous. United States.

13. May, K. T. (2017, April 28). 12 things I know for sure: Anne Lamott speaks at TED2017. TED Blog. Retrieved November 29, 2021, from https://blog.ted.com/12-things-i-know-for-sure-anne-lamott-at-ted2017/.

14. Zukav, Gary. (1989). The Seat of the Soul. Simon & Schuster.

15. Lonsdorf, K., Shapiro, A., & Donevan, C. (2018, June 26). 'a new life': An activist comes home to Zimbabwe, hoping to hold leaders accountable. NPR. Retrieved November 29, 2021, from https://www.npr.org/2018/06/26/623144872/a-new-life-an-activist-comes-home-to-zimbabwe-hoping-to-hold-leaders-accountable.

16. Amateur (n.). Etymology. (n.d.). Retrieved November 29, 2021, from https://www.etymonline.com/word/amateur.

17. Shamsian, J. (2018, April 12). 31 celebrities who found success later in life. Business Insider. Retrieved November 29, 2021, from https://www.businessinsider.com/celebrity-who-became-famous-old-late-bloomer-2018-4.

18. Futterman, M. (2021, September 6). Serena Williams is not at the U.S. Open, but her coach is everywhere. The New York Times. Retrieved November 29, 2021, from https://www.nytimes.com/2021/09/06/sports/tennis/us-open-patrick-mouratoglou.html.

Made in United States
North Haven, CT
21 March 2023

34372819R00075